HEROES OF AMERICAN HISTORY

Abraham Lincoln

The 16th President

Carin T. Ford

Enslow Publishers, Inc.

40 Industrial Road	PO Box 38
Box 398	Aldershot
Berkeley Heights, NJ 07922	Hants GU12 6BP
USA	UK

http://www.enslow.com

Library of Congress Cataloging-in-Publication Data

Ford, Carin T.
   Abraham Lincoln : the 16th president / Carin T. Ford.
      p. cm. — (Heroes of American history)
   Includes index.
   Summary: A biography of our sixteenth president, who guided the nation during its bloodiest fight, the Civil War, and whose life was cut short by an assassin.
   ISBN 0-7660-2000-2 (hardcover)
   1. Lincoln, Abraham, 1809–1865—Juvenile literature. 2. Presidents—United States—Biography—Juvenile literature. [1. Lincoln, Abraham, 1809–1865. 2. Presidents.] I. Title. II. Series.
   E457.905.F66   2002
   973.7'092
   [B]   2002000493

Printed in the United States of America

10 9 8 7 6 5 4 3 2 1

To Our Readers: We have done our best to make sure all Internet Addresses in this book were active and appropriate when we went to press. However, the author and the publisher have no control over and assume no liability for the material available on those Internet sites or on other Web sites they may link to. Any comments or suggestions can be sent by e-mail to comments@enslow.com or to the address on the back cover.

Every effort has been made to locate all copyright holders of material used in this book. If any errors or omissions have occurred, corrections will be made in future editions of this book.

Illustration Credits: © Corel Corporation, p. 1; Illinois State Historical Society, p. 12; Library of Congress, pp. 3, 4, 7, 8, 10, 11, 13, 15, 16 (L), 16 (R), 17, 18, 19, 21, 22, 24, 26, 27, 28; National Archives, p. 23; Painet, Inc., p. 6.

Cover Credits: Library of Congress (portrait); © Corel Corporation (background).

Table of Contents

⭐1 Early Wisdom 5

⭐2 Becoming a Lawyer 9

⭐3 Moving Up. 14

⭐4 16th President 20

⭐5 A Tragic End 25

Timeline. 29

Words to Know 30

Learn More About Abraham Lincoln 31
    (Books and Internet Addresses)

Index. 32

Abraham Lincoln never liked being called Abe.

Chapter 1

Early Wisdom

ight-year-old Abraham Lincoln aimed his rifle at a wild turkey. His family was living in a log cabin in Indiana. It was bitterly cold, and they needed food.

Bang! The turkey was dead, but Abraham was not happy about killing it.

Abraham would always hate killing. Yet when he became president of the United States, he led the nation through its bloodiest fight, the Civil War.

Abraham was born on February 12, 1809, near Hodgenville, Kentucky. He was the second child of Thomas and Nancy Lincoln. Abraham's parents were pioneers in the American West. They were very poor and could not read or write.

In 1816, seven-year-old Abraham and his family moved to Indiana. They worked hard on their new farm. Abraham helped chop down trees to clear the land. He and his family split logs for fences and planted crops such as corn and pumpkins. Even as a

Abraham was born in this log cabin.

boy, Abraham was skilled with an ax. He was tall and strong.

When Abraham was nine, his mother died. The next year, Thomas Lincoln found a new wife. Sarah was a widow with three children. She became a kind, loving mother to Abraham and his sister.

Sarah made sure all the children went to school. Abraham was a quiet, polite student. Everyone looked up to him. When there was trouble, they turned to Abraham to settle the problem.

Abraham loved his stepmother, Sarah, very much.

Abraham loved to read. He wanted to spend all his time with his books. But his father thought reading was a waste of time. He needed Abraham to help out on the farm.

So Abraham attended school "by littles," he said.

He went just a few weeks at a time. His total schooling added up to less than a year.

Still, Abraham always had a book with him. When he took a break from plowing the fields, Abraham liked to sit down under a tree and read.

Abraham enjoyed reading books and writing poetry.

Chapter 2

Becoming a Lawyer

A braham grew taller and stronger every year. Soon he was six feet four inches tall and an excellent athlete.

He had a gift for telling jokes and was well known as a storyteller. Although Abraham often had times when he felt gloomy, he loved to laugh.

In 1830, the Lincoln family moved to Illinois. Abraham drove one of the ox-drawn wagons and

Abraham floated his flatboat down the river carrying farm goods to market.

helped his father build a cabin on the prairie.

The next year, when Abraham was twenty-two, he left home. He wanted to strike out on his own. He worked on a flatboat that traveled down the Mississippi River.

When Abraham returned, he took a job in a general store in New Salem, Illinois. He was shy and very poor. He did not have a coat, and his pants were five inches too short.

But Abraham was honest and friendly. He enjoyed talking with the customers, especially about politics. In 1832, he ran for state legislature, which is the lawmaking part of the government. He lost

Abraham was known for his skill at splitting logs
to make fence rails.

the election. During the next couple of years, he served for a short time as a soldier, was part owner of a general store, and became the local postmaster.

Abraham ran for state legislature again in 1834. This time he won. Over the years, he was reelected for three more terms.

At his general store, Abraham sold everything from dishes and tools to tea and sweets.

At that time, lawmakers earned $3 a day. It was not enough to live on, so Abraham needed another job, too. He decided he would like to be a lawyer.

As a lawmaker and a lawyer, Abraham worked many hours at the State House in Springfield.

Abraham borrowed law books and studied whenever he had spare time. He even read while he was walking down the street. Abraham's favorite place to study was outdoors, where he leaned against a tree, barefoot.

When Abraham was twenty-eight, he passed his exam to become a lawyer. He soon became known for speaking plainly and always getting to the heart of the matter.

Chapter 3

Moving Up

braham moved to Springfield, Illinois, to open his law office. He rode into town on a horse he had borrowed. He had only $7 in his pocket.

Abraham rented a room above a general store. When he finished work for the day, Abraham liked to sit at the back of the store and swap stories with the townsfolk.

Abraham also fell in love. Mary Todd was wealthy

and well educated. Mary's family did not want her to marry Abraham. He became very sad. He did not see Mary for more than a year.

Then, in 1842, the couple met again. They still loved each other and decided to get married. Over time, they had four sons, Robert, Edward, William, and Thomas.

Still, Mary and Abraham were very different from each other. Mary liked to argue and say what was on her mind. Abraham did

Abraham's law office was in downtown Springfield, Illinois. It was in the building marked with an X.

Abraham was 33 years old when he married Mary, age 23.

not like quarreling. Mary liked fine clothes. Abraham often wore shirts and pants that did not match.

Mary did not understand Abraham's moods. She also did not know how he could become so lost in thought. Once, he was pulling a wagon along the street with one of their sons in it. Abraham did not notice when the wagon tipped and the boy fell out. Abraham kept walking, pulling the empty wagon behind him.

Four years after his marriage, Abraham was elected to Congress. The Lincolns moved to the nation's capital, Washington, D.C., in 1847. Abraham was a congressman for two years. Then he returned to Springfield and went back to being a lawyer.

Abraham's office was messy. Books and letters were scattered everywhere. He kept bills and papers in his tall stovepipe hat. They often tumbled to the ground when he took it off his head!

Many people hired Abraham as their lawyer. He took all sorts of cases—murders, fights over property,

Abraham spoke very well in court. He was one of the best lawyers in Illinois.

even arguments about pigs. Abraham worked for all kinds of people, from very rich to very poor.

In 1858, Abraham ran for U.S. Senate. He lost the election, but the speeches he gave made him well known.

All his life, Abraham hated slave markets and slavery.

One of the important ideas Abraham talked about was slavery. In the southern states, many people used slaves to work in the fields and do housework. Slaves had no rights. They could be bought and sold because they were thought of as property—not as people. Almost 4 million slaves lived in the South.

Abraham, along with many people in the North,

The Lincoln family at home.

was against slavery. "If slavery is not wrong, nothing is wrong," he said.

Abraham kept making speeches throughout the North. People began to think he would be a good leader for the country. In 1860, Abraham was chosen to run for president of the United States.

Chapter 4

16th President

Abraham was elected president of the United States on November 6, 1860. He faced serious problems right away. Before he even took office, eleven southern states broke away from the rest of the country.

The people in these states were worried that the new president would put an end to slavery. They wanted to be a separate nation so they could keep

Many people called Abraham "Honest Abe" because he was always so truthful.

their slaves. They called themselves the Confederate States of America.

In April 1861, Confederate soldiers attacked a South Carolina fort that belonged to the United States government. Fort Sumter did not have many men or supplies. It was forced to surrender to the southern soldiers.

Abraham had hoped to avoid war. But now he called for 75,000 men to join the U.S. Army.

The attack on Fort Sumter in Charleston started the Civil War.

It was North against South; American against American. The Civil War had begun.

Abraham did not think the war would last very long. The North had more men, more money, and more factories making guns.

Yet the Civil War dragged on. The war had been started to save the United States—to keep the North and South

President Lincoln visited the battlefield.

together as one country. After a while, President Lincoln realized the real problem was slavery.

In 1863, he wrote an important paper called the Emancipation Proclamation. It stated that all slaves in the South were now "forever free." "If my name ever goes into history, it will be for this act," he said.

Abraham believed that all people should be free.

Chapter 5

A Tragic End

he Civil War had been going on for about two years when the North finally began winning some important battles. In July 1863, northern soldiers defeated the South in Gettysburg, Pennsylvania. More than 50,000 men were hurt, missing, or killed in the war's bloodiest battle.

Abraham gave a speech to honor the soldiers who

A terrible battle took place near the little town of Gettysburg, Pennsylvania.

had fought at Gettysburg. He said these men had died there so the "nation might live."

The speech was very short—less than three minutes. Abraham thought it was a failure. Yet the Gettysburg Address has become one of the most famous speeches in our country's history.

Abraham was elected for another term as president. But the war had been hard on his health. He did not seem well.

Finally, on April 9, 1865, the Civil War ended. It had lasted four years. More than 600,000 men had died. Millions of slaves had won their freedom, and the nation would stay united.

Five nights after the South surrendered, Abraham went to Ford's Theater in Washington, D.C. While he was watching a play, the president was shot by John Wilkes Booth. He was an actor who had wanted the South to win the war.

Booth then escaped by horseback to Virginia.

Abraham was shot while sitting in a theater watching a play.

Government soldiers found and killed him twelve days later in a barn.

With a bullet in his head, Abraham was barely breathing. He was taken to a house across the street from the theater. Doctors could not save him. The president died on the morning of April 15, 1865.

As the train carried Abraham's body back to Springfield, Illinois, thousands of people gathered at each stop. They brought poems and flowers to honor him.

Abraham Lincoln became a great man through hard work and a strong belief in doing what was right. As president of the United States, he helped unite the country and free the slaves.

Timeline

1809~Born near Hodgenville, Kentucky, on February 12.

1830~Moves to Illinois.

1834~Is elected to the Illinois state legislature.

1837~Begins practicing law in Springfield, Illinois.

1842~Marries Mary Todd.

1846~Is elected to Congress.

1860~Becomes the 16th president of the United States.

1863~Signs the Emancipation Proclamation.

1864~Is reelected president for a second term.

1865~Is shot by John Wilkes Booth and dies the next day, April 15.

Words to Know

Civil War—In the United States, the Civil War was fought between northern states and southern states from 1861 to 1865.

Confederate States of America—The eleven states that wanted to be a separate nation: Alabama, Arkansas, Florida, Georgia, Louisiana, Mississippi, North Carolina, South Carolina, Tennessee, Texas, and Virginia.

Emancipation Proclamation—A ruling written by President Lincoln that freed all the slaves in the southern states.

Gettysburg Address—A famous speech given by President Lincoln during the Civil War.

legislature—The lawmaking part of the government.

pioneers—The people who are first to settle in an area.

politics—The workings of government.

U.S. Congress—The national legislature of the United States. It has two parts, the Senate and the House of Representatives.

Learn More

Books

Brenner, Martha. *Abe Lincoln's Hat.* New York: Random House, 1994.

Fontes, Ron, and Justine Korman. *Abraham Lincoln: Lawyer, Leader, Legend.* New York: Dorling Kindersley, 2001.

Harness, Cheryl. *Abe Lincoln Goes to Washington.* Washington, D.C.: National Geographic Society, 1997.

Internet Addresses

Excellent photographs of Lincoln and his family
<http://www.chicagohistory.org/AOTM/feb99/feb99fact2a.html>

An award-winning site with activities and links
<http://www.siec.k12.in.us/~west/proj/lincoln/index.html>

Abraham Lincoln Online
<http://showcase.netins.net/web/creative/lincoln.html>

The Civil War
<http://www.historyplace.com>

Index

B

Booth, John Wilkes, 27

C

Civil War, 5, 22–27
Confederate States of America, 22

E

Emancipation Proclamation, 23, 24

F

Ford's Theater, 27
Fort Sumter, 22

G

Gettysburg, Pennsylvania, 25–26
Gettysburg Address, 26

H

Hodgenville, Kentucky, 6

L

Lincoln, Abraham
  birth, 6
  childhood, 5–8
  congressman, 16–17
  death, 28
  early jobs, 10, 12
  education, 7–8
  lawmaker, 10, 12
  lawyer, 12, 13, 14, 17–18
  marriage, 15
  president, 20–28
  views on slavery, 18–19
Lincoln, Edward (son), 15
Lincoln, Mary Todd (wife), 14–16
Lincoln, Nancy (mother), 6, 7
Lincoln, Robert (son), 15

Lincoln, Sarah (stepmother), 7
Lincoln, Thomas (father), 6, 7, 10
Lincoln, Thomas (son), 15
Lincoln, William (son), 15

M

Mississippi River, 10

N

New Salem, Illinois, 10

S

slavery, 18, 20, 23, 27
Springfield, Illinois, 13, 14, 15, 28

W

Washington, D.C., 17, 27